C c K k

Some Spanish dancers are performing. The ladies wear bright dresses and click castanets, *ck, ck, ck, ck*.

Action: Snap your fingers together in the air as if you are playing castanets, and say *c, k, ck, ck*.

The letters ‹c› and ‹k› make the same sound. To help remember the different shapes, we call them:

caterpillar /c/

kicking /k/

cap

kick

cat

stick

Snake is very fond of eggs. He cracks them open, *e, e, e, egg.* Inky and Bee prefer chocolate eggs!

E e

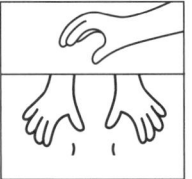

Action: Pretend to crack an egg against the side of a pan with one hand. Use both hands to open the shell, saying *e, e, e, e.*

Help hen get to her eggs. Keep inside the lines.

e

e e e e e e e

e e e e e e e

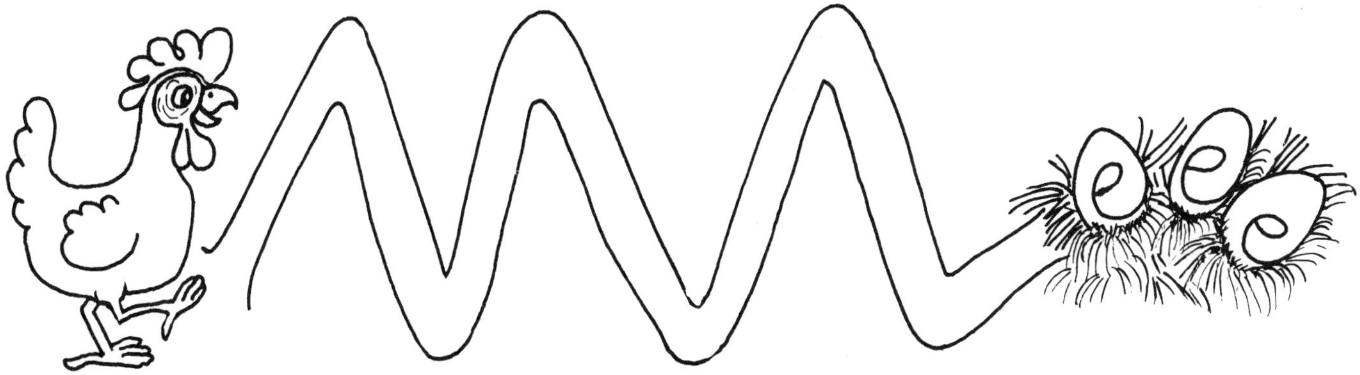

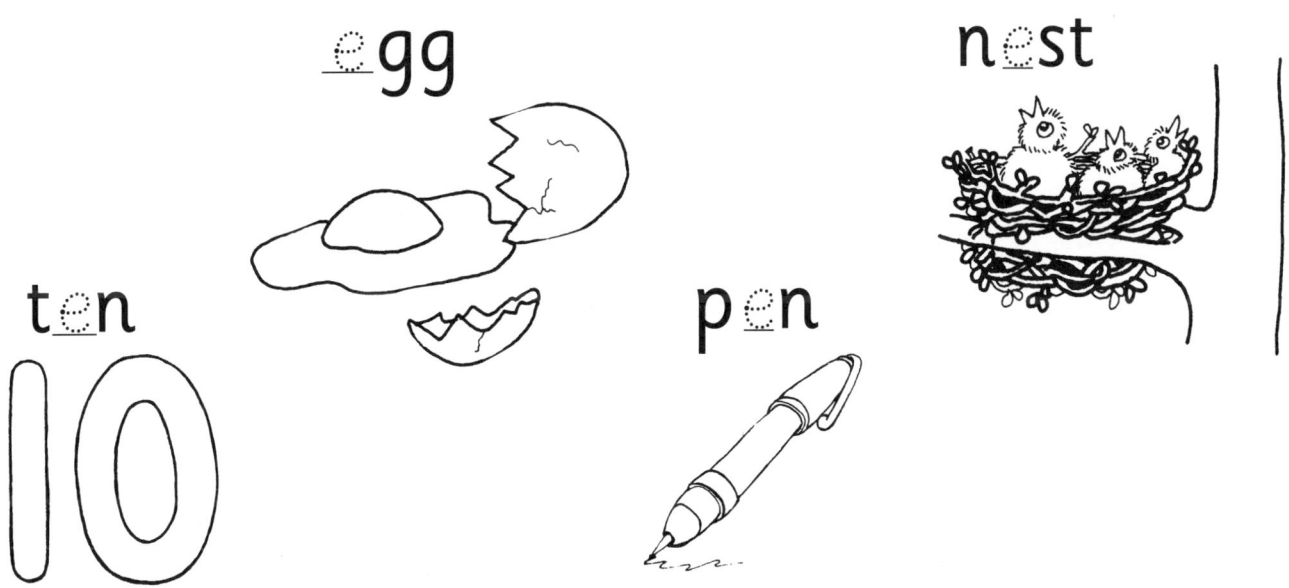

egg

nest

ten

pen

H h

Inky and Bee are having a hopping race. When they finish they are hot and tired, huffing *h, h, h.*

Action: Hold your hand up to your mouth as if you are out of breath, and say *h, h, h, h.*

Help frog hop to his lily pad. Keep inside the lines.

h

h h h h h h h h
h h h h h h h h

hiss

hand

hen

hat

R r

The puppy has a special piece of rag. He holds on to it and pulls, shaking his head and growling *rrrrrr*.

Action: Pretend to be a puppy pulling a rag and shake your head from side to side, saying *rrrrr*.

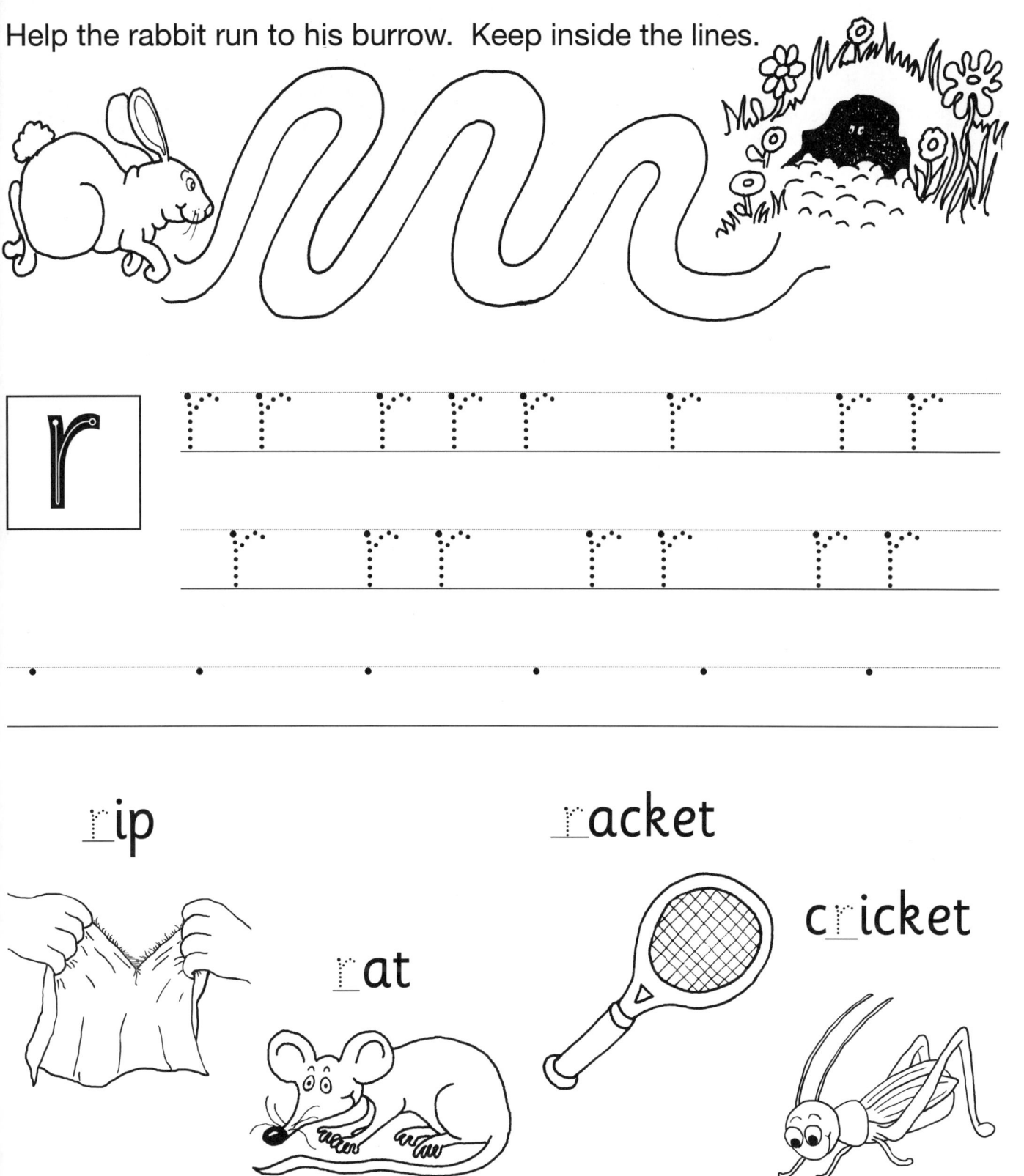

Snake likes to eat eggs best of all. Inky prefers cheese and Bee likes honey. When they see their food they rub their tummies and say *mmmmmm.*

Action: Rub your tummy as if you can see some tasty food, and say *mmmmmm*.

Help mole get back to his molehill. Keep inside the lines.

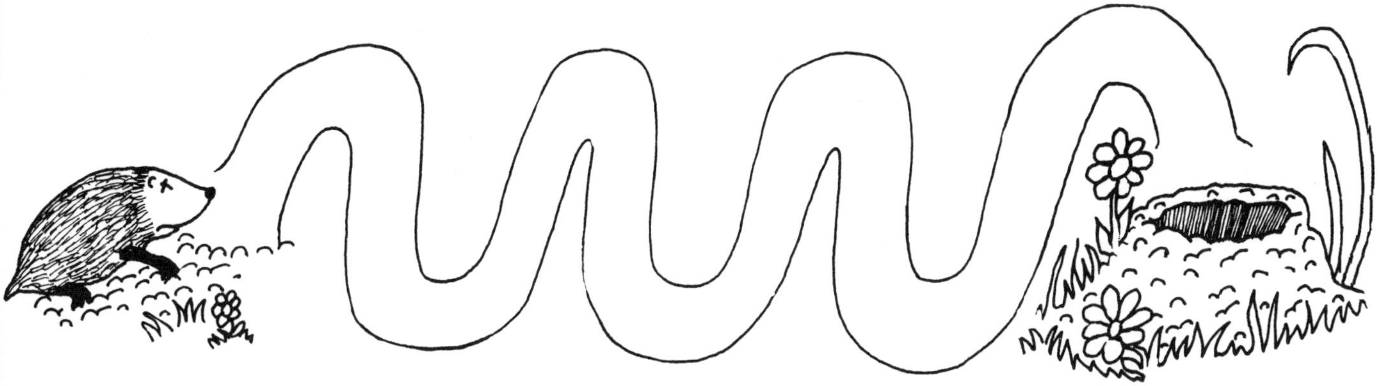

m m. m. m. m. m.

m. m. m. m. m.

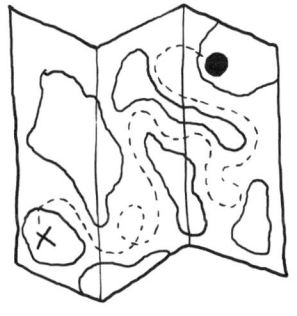
m ap

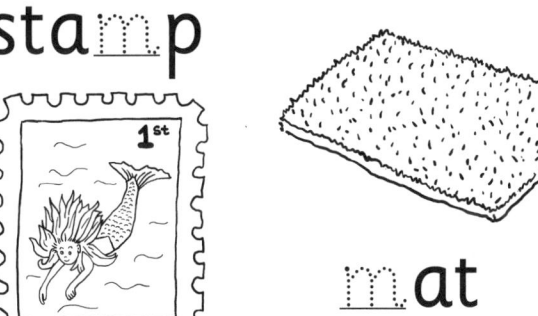
sta m p

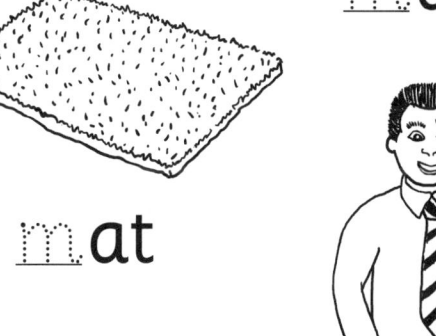
m at

m an

Inky, Snake and Bee have found an old toy drum. They all have a go at banging the drum, *d, d, d, d.*

D d

Action: Move your hands up and down as if you are beating a drum, and say *d, d, d, d*.

Take the dog back to his kennel. Keep inside the lines.

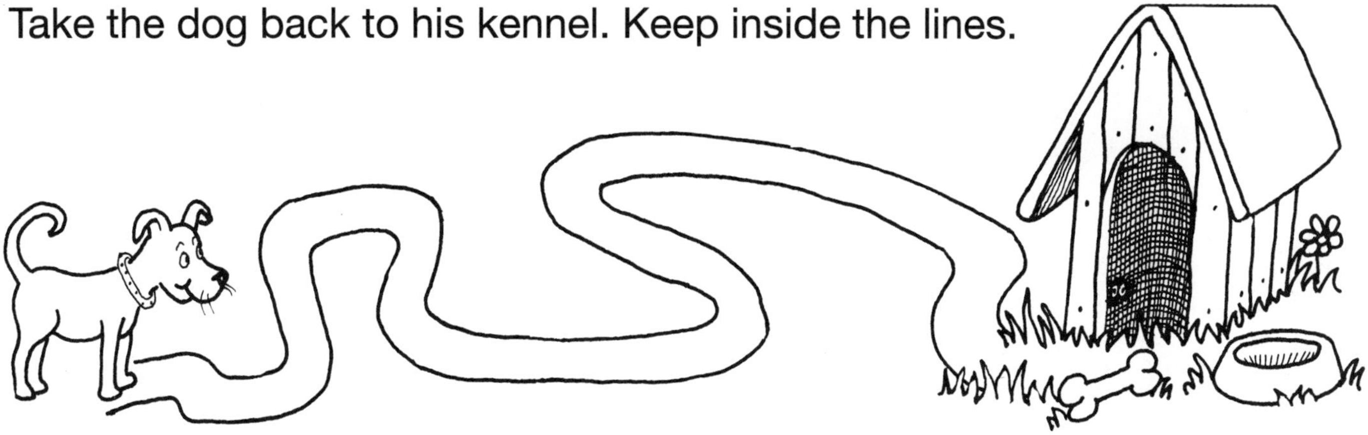

d

d d d d d

d d d d d d d d

dress

hand

drink

desk

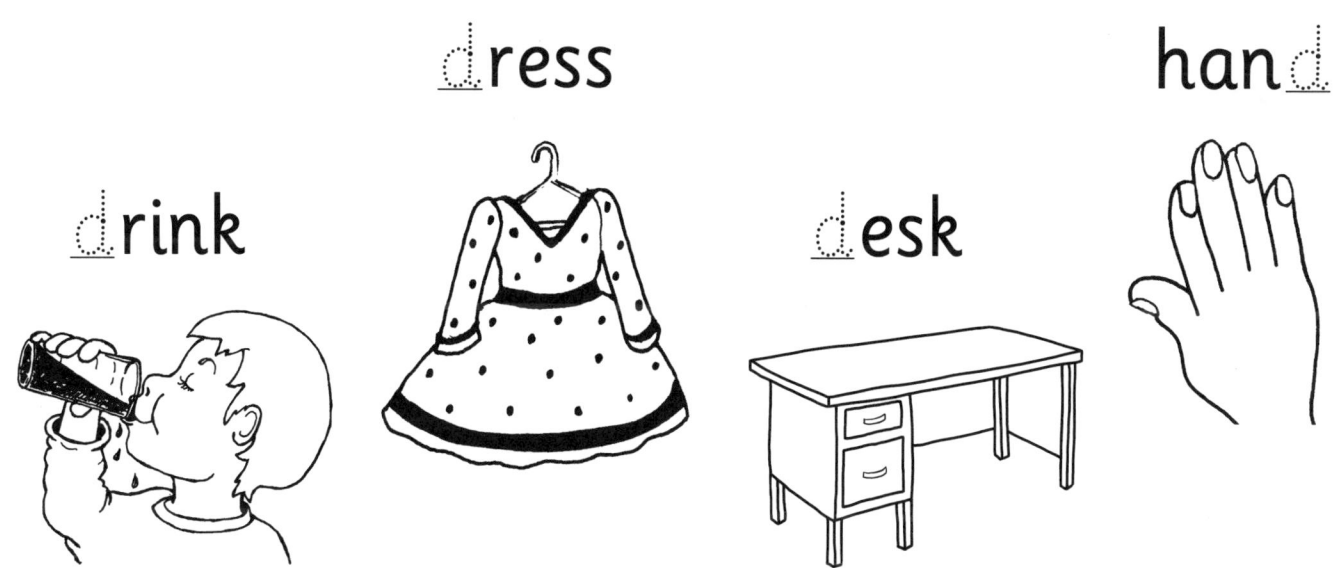

Join each picture to the letter for the sound it begins with.

Practise the ‹c› shape.
Caterpillar /c/

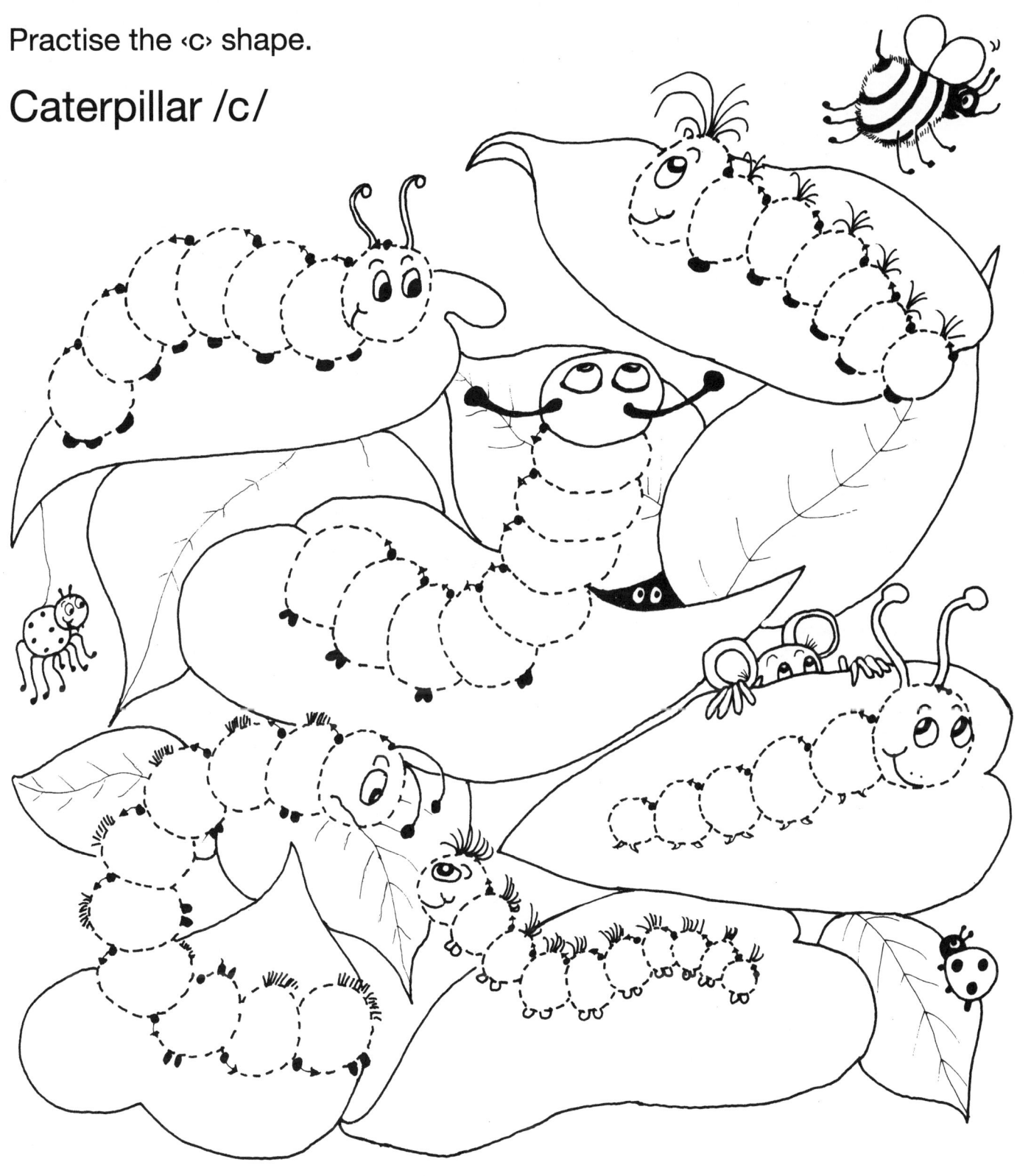

Write the letter for the sound at the end of each word.

✂ How to make this book:
1. Cut along the dotted lines.
2. Put the top sheet on top of the other. Fold in half.

Note: This book is intended for use when the children have completed this workbook, including reading double sounds (/ck/, /tt/ etc.).

Rats!

②

⑦

Red hen pecks at a sack.

④

A cat and a kitten.

⑤

Red Hen

①

Red hen sits and rests.

⑧

Red hen has hidden in a sack.
Kitten pats it.

⑥

Red hen sits on a nest.

③

When two letters that make the same sound come together, as with ‹c› and ‹k›, you only say the sound once. Trace over the letters, read the word and draw a picture.

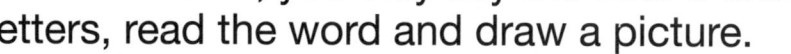

Write in the missing letters. Then read the word and draw a picture in the space.

Trace over the dotted lines.

Can you hear the sound in the words? In each row, cross out the picture of the word without that sound.

1 2

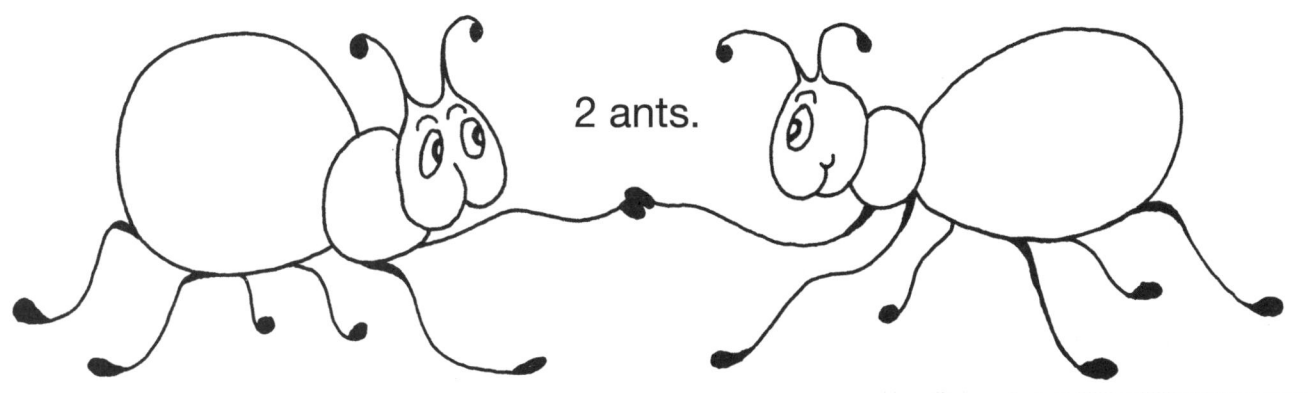

2 ants.

Trace over the dotted lines to write the number 2.

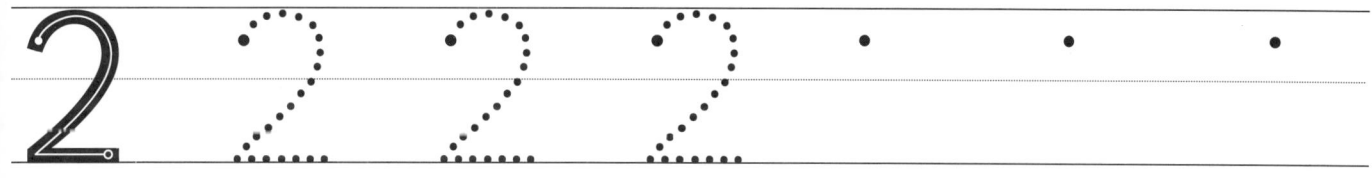

Find the 2 ants.

Activity

Eggs-panding hair!
Stand half an egg shell in a pot and give it a face. Put in some damp cotton balls or paper. Sprinkle some cress or other small seeds onto it. Wait for a few days and watch the 'hair' grow!

Mmmm meal
Stick pictures of tasty food onto a paper plate.

Edible letters
Make the mixture for some plain cookies or biscuits. Cut out letter shapes from a piece of card. Put the letter shapes onto the rolled-out mix and cut around them.

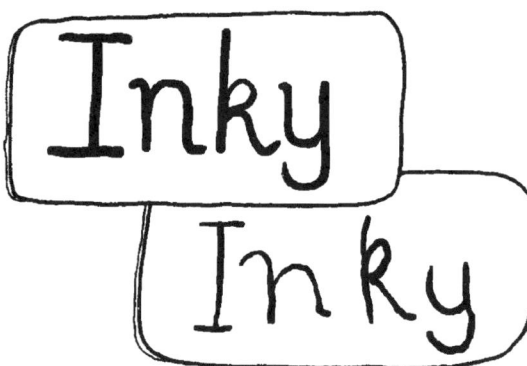

Name card
Get an adult to write your name for you. Cut out a piece of card, about 10cm by 20cm. Copy your name onto the card.